MASSACHUSETTS IN MOURNING.

A

SERMON,

PREACHED

IN WORCESTER, ON SUNDAY, JUNE 4, 1854.

BY

THOMAS WENTWORTH HIGGINSON,
Minister of the Worcester Free Church.

REPRINTED, BY REQUEST, FROM THE WORCESTER DAILY SPY.

BOSTON:
JAMES MUNROE AND COMPANY.
1854.

BOSTON:
PRESS OF PRENTISS AND SAWYER,
No. 19 Water Street.

SERMON.

Shall the iron break the Northern iron and the steel? — JEREMIAH xv. 12.

You have imagined my subject beforehand, for there is but one subject on which I could preach, or you could listen, to-day. Yet, how hard it is to say one word of that. You do not ask, at a funeral, that the bereaved mourners themselves should speak, but you call in one a little farther removed, to utter words of comfort, if comfort there be. But to-day is, or should be, to every congregation in Massachusetts, a day of funeral service — we are all mourners — and what is there for me to say?

Yet, even in this gloom, the faculty of wonder is left; as at funerals, men ask in a low tone, around the coffin, what was the disease that smote this fair form, and are we safe from the infection? So we now ask, what is lost, and how have we lost it, and what have we left? Is it all gone, (men say,) that old New England heroism and enthusiasm? Is there any disinterested love of Freedom left in Massachusetts? And then they think with joy, (as I do,) that, at least, Freedom did not die without a struggle, and that it took thousands of armed men to lay her in the grave at last.

I am thankful for all this. Words are nothing — we have been surfeited with words for twenty years. I am thankful that this time there was action also ready for Freedom. God gave men bodies, to live and work in; the powers of those bodies are the first things to be consecrated to the Right. He gave us higher powers, also, for weapons, but, in using those, we must not forget to hold the lower ones also ready; else we miss our proper manly life on earth, and lay down our means of usefulness before we have outgrown them. "Render unto Cæsar the things which are Cæsar's and unto God the things which are God's." Our souls and bodies are both God's, and resistance to tyrants is obedience to Him.

If you meet men whose souls are contaminated, and have time enough to work on them, you can deal with them by the weapons of the soul alone; but if men array brute force against Freedom — pistols, clubs, drilled soldiers, and stone walls — then the body also has its part to do in resistance. You must hold yourself above men, I own, yet not too far above to reach them.

I do not like even to think of taking life, only of giving it; but physical force that is forcible enough, acts without bloodshed. They say that with twenty more men at hand, that Friday night, at the Boston Court House, the Slave might have been rescued without even the death of that one man — who was perhaps killed by his frightened companions, then and there. So you see force may not mean bloodshed; and calm, irresistible force, in a good cause, becomes sublime. The strokes on the door of that Court House that night for instance — they may perchance have disturbed some dreamy saint from his meditations, (if dreamy saints abound in Court Square,) — but I think they went echoing from town to town, from Boston to far New Orleans, like the first drum beat of the Revolution — and each reverberating throb was a blow upon the door of every Slave-prison of this guilty Republic.

That first faint throb of Liberty was a proud thing for Boston; Boston which was a scene so funereal a week after. Men say the act of one Friday helped prepare for the next; I am glad if it did. If the attack on the Court House had no greater effect than to send that Slave away under a guard of two thousand men, instead of two hundred, it was worth a dozen lives. If we are all Slaves indeed — if there is no law in Massachusetts except the telegraphic orders from Washington — if our own military are to be made Slave-catchers — if our Governor is a mere piece of State ceremony, permitted only to rise at a military dinner and thank his own soldiers for their readiness to shoot down his own constituents, without even the delay of a riot act — if Massachusetts is merely a conquered province and under martial law — *then I wish to know it,* and I am grateful for every additional gun and sabre that forces the truth deeper into our hearts. *Lower, Massachusetts, lower, kneel still lower!* Serve, Irish Marines! the kidnappers, your masters; down in the dust, citizen soldiery! before the Irish Marines, and for you, O Governor, a lower humility yet, and your homage must be paid, at second hand, before the stained and soiled "citizen soldiery."

I remember the great trades-procession in Boston, a few years since, in honor of the visitors from the North, from the free soil of Canada. Then all choice implements, which Massachusetts had invented to supply the industry of the world, were brought forth for exhibition, and superb was the show. This time we had visitors from the South — the South which uses tools also — and imports them all, "hoes, spades, axes, politicians, and ministers." So the last new implements, for her use, were to be exhibited now. There were twenty-one specimens of Boston military companies. There were the two hundred more confidential bullies, for whom the city was ransacked, men so vile, that it was said the police had no duties left, for all the dangerous persons were employed as policemen themselves, — men whom a Police Judge having inspected, recognized criminal after criminal, who had been sentenced by himself to the House of Correction; these came next. Truly as there is joy in heaven over one sinner who repenteth, so there was joy in Boston that day, over one sinner who had not repented, — over every man in whom the powers of hell were strong enough, aided by public brandy, to fit him for that terrible service. Those were the tools marshalled forth for exhibition. But why were these only shown? Why were the finer, the more precious implements kept invisible that day, the real engines of that Slaveholder's triumph? Why not make the picture perfect? Place, O Chief Marshal, between the Slave and the guardian cannon, the crowning glory of that sad procession, the Slaveholder in his carriage, and chain, on the one side, the Mayor of Boston, and, on the other side, the Governor of the Commonwealth, with the motto, "The Representative Men of Massachusetts, — *These tools she gives, Virginia, to thee!*"

I mean no personality. The men who occupy these offices, are men who (I have always thought) did them honor. I suppose that neither would own a Slave, nor (personally) catch one. No doubt they favorably represent the average of Massachusetts men. *But I introduce them for precisely this reason,* to show the tragedy of our American institutions, that they take average Massachusetts men, put them into public office, and then, demanding more of them than their education gives them manliness to meet, — use them, crush them, and drop them, into the dishonor with which these hitherto honored men are suddenly overwhelmed to-day.

If such be the influence of our national organization, what good do our efforts do? Our labor to reform the North, with the whole force of nationalized Slavery to resist, is like the effort of Sir John Franklin, on his first voyage, to get northward by travelling on the ice. He travelled toward the pole for six weeks, no doubt of that; but at the end of the time he was two hundred miles farther from it than when he started. The ice had floated southward — *and our ice floats southward also.* And so it will be, while this Union concentrates power in the hands of Slaveholders, and gives the North only commercial prosperity, the more thoroughly to enervate and destroy it.

Here, for instance, is the Nebraska Emigration Society; it is indeed, a noble enterprise, and I am proud that it owes its origin to a Worcester man — but where is the good of emigrating to Nebraska, if Nebraska is to be only a transplanted Massachusetts, and the original Massachusetts has been tried and found wanting? Will the stream rise higher than its source? Settle your Nebraska ten years, and you will have your New England harvest of corn and grain, more luxuriant in that virgin soil; — ah, but will not the other Massachusetts crop come also, of political demagogues and wire-pullers, and a sectarian religion, which will insure the passage of the greatest hypocrite to heaven, if he will join the right church before he goes? And give the emigrants twenty years more of prosperity, and then ask them, if you dare, to break law and disturb order, and risk life, merely to save their State from the shame that has just blighted Massachusetts?

In view of these facts, what stands between us and a military despotism? "Sure guarantees," you say. So has every nation thought until its fall came. "The outward form of Roman institutions stood uninjured till long after Caligula had made his horse consul." What is your safeguard? Nothing but a parchment Constitution, which has been riddled through and through whenever it pleased the Slave Power; which has not been able to preserve to you the oldest privileges of Freedom — Habeas Corpus and Trial by Jury! Stranger still, that men should think to find a security in our material prosperity, and our career of foreign conquest, and our acquisition of gold mines, and forget that these have been precisely the symptoms which have prophesied the decline of every powerful commercial state — Rome, Carthage, Tyre, Venice, Spain, Holland, and all the rest.

In the third century after the birth of Jesus, Terullian painted that brilliant picture of the Roman power, which describes us, as if it were written for us:

"Certainly," says he, "the world becomes more and more our tributary; none of its secret recesses have remained inaccessible, all are known, frequented, and all have become the scene or the object of traffic. Who now dreads an unknown island? who trembles at a reef? our ships are sure to be met with everywhere — everywhere is a people, a state; everywhere is life. We crush the world beneath our weight — *onerosi sumus mundo.*"

And Rome perished, almost when the words were uttered!

How simple the acts of our tragedy may be! Let another Fugitive Slave case occur, and more blood be spilt (as might happen another time;) — let Massachusetts be declared insurrectionary, and placed under martial law, (as it might;) — let the President be made Dictator, with absolute power; let him send his willing Attorney General to buy up officers of militia, (which would be easy,) and frighten Officers of State, (which would be easier;) — let him get half the press, and a quarter of the pulpits, to sustain his usurpation, under the name of "law and order"; — let the flame spread from New England to New York, from New York to Ohio, from Ohio to Wisconsin; — and how long would it take for some future Franklin Pierce to stand where Louis Napoleon stands now? How much would the commercial leaders of the East resist, if an appeal were skilfully made to their pockets? — or the political demagogues of the West, if an appeal were made to their ambition? It seems inconceivable! Certainly — so did the *coup d'etat* of Louis Napoleon, the day before it happened!

"Do not despair of the Republic," says some one, remembering the hopeful old Roman motto. But they had to despair of that one in the end, — and why not of this one also? Why, when we were going on, step by step, as older Republics have done, should we expect to stop just as we reach the brink of Niagara? The love of Liberty grows stronger every year, some think, in some places. Thirty years ago, it cost only $25 to restore a Fugitive Slave from Boston, and now it costs $100,000; — *but still the Slave is restored.* I know there are thousands of hearts which stand pledged to Liberty now, and these may save the State, in spite of her officials and her military; but can they save the Nation? They may give us disunion instead of despotism, but can they give us anything better? Can they even give us anything so good?

We talk of the Anti-Slavery sentiment as being stronger ; but in spite of your Free Soil votes, your Uncle Tom's Cabin, and your New York Tribunes, here is the simple fact: *the South beats us more and more easily every time.* So chess-players, when they have once or twice overcome a weak antagonist, think it safe, next time, to give up to him a half dozen pieces by way of odds ;—and after all gain the victory. Compare this Nebraska game with the previous ones. The Slave Power could afford to give us the Whig party on our side, this time—could give up to us the commercial influence of Boston and New York, so strong an ally before—it has not had the name and presence of Daniel Webster to help it now, nor the voices of clergymen, nor the terror of disunion, nor the weariness after a long Anti-Slavery excitement: it has dispensed with all these ;—nay, the whole contest was on our own soil, to defend the poor little landmark we had retreated to long before ;—and for all this, the Slave Power has conquered us, just as easily as it conquered us on Texas, Mexico, and the compromises of 1850.

No wonder that this excitement is turning Whigs and Democrats into Free Soilers, and Free Soilers into disunionists. But this is only the eddy, after all; the main current sets the wrong way. The nation is intoxicated and depraved. It takes all the things you count as influential,—all the "spirit of the age," and the "moral sentiment of Christendom," and the best eloquence and literature of the time,—to balance the demoralization of a single term of Presidential patronage. Give the offices of the nation to be controlled by the Slave Power, and I tell you that there is not one in ten, even of professed Anti-Slavery men, who can stand the fire in that furnace of sin ; and there is not a plot so wicked

but it will have, like all its predecessors, a sufficient majority when the time comes.

Do you doubt this? Name, if you can, a victory of Freedom, or a defeat of the Slave Power, within twenty years, except on the right of petition, and even that was only a recovery of lost ground. Do you say, the politicians are false, but the people mark the men who betray them! True, they mark them, but as merchants mark goods, with the cost price, that they may raise the price a little, when they want to sell the same article again. You must go back to the original Missouri Compromise, if you wish to prove that even Massachusetts punishes traitors to Freedom, by any severer penalty than a seat on her Supreme Bench. For myself, I do not believe in these Anti-Slavery spasms of our people, for the same reason that Coleridge did not believe in ghosts, because I have seen too many of them myself. I remember when our Massachusetts delegation in Congress, signed a sort of threat that the State would withdraw from the Union if Texas came in, but it never happened. I remember the State Convention at Faneuil Hall in 1845, where the lion and the lamb lay down together, and George T. Curtis and John G. Whittier were Secretaries; and the Convention solemnly pronounced the annexation of Texas to be "the overthrow of the Constitution, the bond of the existing Union." I remember how one speaker boasted that if Texas was voted in by joint resolution, it might be voted out by the same. But somehow, we have never mustered that amount of resolution; and when I hear of State Street petitioning for the repeal of its own Fugitive Slave Law, I remember the lesson.

For myself, I do not expect to live to see that law repealed by the votes of politicians at Washington. It can only be repealed by ourselves, upon the soil of Massachusetts. For one, I am glad to be deceived no longer. I am glad of the discovery — (no hasty thing, but gradually dawning upon me for ten years) — that I live under a despotism. I have lost the dream that ours is a land of peace and order. I have looked thoroughly through our "Fourth of July," and seen its hollowness; and I advise you to petition your City Government to revoke their appropriation for its celebration, (or give the same to the Nebraska Emigration Society,) and only toll the bells in all the churches, and hang the streets in black from end to end. O shall we hold such ceremonies when only some statesman is gone, and omit them over dead Freedom, whom all true statesmen only live to serve!

At any rate my word of counsel to you is to learn this lesson thoroughly — *a revolution is begun!* not a Reform, but a Revolution. If you take part in politics henceforward, let it be only to bring nearer the crisis which will either save or sunder this nation — or perhaps save in sundering. I am not very hopeful, even as regards you; I know the mass of men will not make great sacrifices for Freedom, but there is more need of those who will. I have lost faith forever in numbers; I have faith only in the constancy and courage of a "forlorn hope." And for aught we know, a case may arise, this week, in Massachusetts, which may not end like the last one.

Let us speak the truth. Under the influence of Slavery, we are rapidly relapsing into that state of barbarism in which every man must rely on his own right hand for his protection. Let any man yield to his instinct of Freedom, and resist oppression, and his life is at the mercy of the first drunken officer who orders his troops to fire. For myself, existence looks worthless under such circumstances; and I can only make life worth living for, by becoming a revolutionist. The saying seems dangerous; but why not say it if one means it, as I certainly do. I respect law and order, but as the ancient Persian sage said, "*always* to obey the laws, virtue must relax much of her vigor." I see, now, that while Slavery is national, law and order must constantly be on the wrong side. I see that the case stands for me precisely as it stands for Kossuth and Mazzini, and I must take the consequences.

Do you say that ours is a Democratic Government, and there is a more peaceable remedy? I deny that we live under a Democracy. It is an oligarchy of Slaveholders, and I point to the history of a half century to prove it. Do you say, that oligarchy will be propitiated by submission? I deny it. It is the plea of the timid in all ages. Look at the experience of our own country. Which is most influential in Congress — South Carolina, which never submitted to anything, or Massachusetts, with thrice the white population, but which always submits to everything? I tell you, there is not a free State in the Union which would dare treat a South Carolinian as that State treated Mr. Hoar; or, if it had been done, the Union would have been divided years ago. The way to make principles felt is to assert them — peaceably, if you can; forcibly, if you must. The way to promote Free Soil is to have your own soil free; to leave courts to settle constitutions, and to fall back (for your own part,) on first principles: then it will be seen that you mean something. How much free territory is there beneath the Stars and Stripes? I know of four places — Syracuse, Wilkesbarre, Milwaukie, and Chicago: I remember no others. "Worcester," you say. Worcester has not yet been tried. If you

think Worcester County is free, say so and act accordingly. Call a County Convention, and declare that you leave legal quibbles to lawyers, and parties to politicians, and plant yourselves on the simple truth that God never made a Slave, and that man shall neither make nor take one here! Over your own city, at least, you have power; but will you stand the test when it comes? Then do not try to avoid it. For one thing only I blush — that a Fugitive has ever fled from here to Canada. Let it not happen again, I charge you, if you are what you think you are. No longer conceal Fugitives and help them on, but show them and defend them. Let the Underground Railroad stop here! Say to the South that Worcester, though a part of a Republic, shall be as free as if ruled by a Queen! *Hear, O Richmond! and give ear, O Carolina! henceforth Worcester is Canada to the Slave!* And what will Worcester be to the kidnapper? I dare not tell; and I fear that the poor sinner himself, if once recognized in our streets, would scarcely get back to tell the tale.

I do not discourage more peaceable instrumentalities; would to God that no other were ever needful. Make laws, if you can, though you have State processes already, if you had officers to enforce them; and, indeed, what can any State process do, except to legalize nullification? Use politics, if you can make them worth using, though a coalition administration proved as powerless, in the Sims case, as a Whig administration has proved now. But the disease lies deeper than these remedies can reach. It is all idle to try to save men by law and order, merely, while the men themselves grow selfish and timid, and are only ready to talk of Liberty, and risk nothing for it. Our people have no active physical habits; their intellects are sharpened, but their bodies, and even their hearts, are left untrained; they learn only (as a French satirist once said,) the fear of God and the love of money; they are taught that they owe the world nothing, but that the world owes them a living, and so they make a living; but the fresh, strong spirit of Liberty droops and decays, and only makes a dying. I charge you, parents, do not be so easily satisfied; encourage nobler instincts in your children, and appeal to nobler principles; teach your daughter that life is something more than dress and show, and your son that there is some nobler aim in existence than a good bargain, and a fast horse, and an oyster supper. Let us have the brave, simple instincts of Circassian mountaineers, without their ignorance; and the unfaltering moral courage of the Puritans, without their superstition; so that we may show the world that a community may be educated in brain without becoming cowardly in body; and that a people without a standing army may yet rise as one man, when Freedom needs defenders.

May God help us so to redeem this oppressed and bleeding State, and to bring this people back to that simple love of Liberty, without which it must die amidst its luxuries, like the sad nations of the elder world. May we gain more iron in our souls, and have it in the right place;—have soft hearts and hard wills, not as now, soft wills and hard hearts. Then will the iron break the Northern iron and the steel no longer; and "God save the Commonwealth of Massachusetts!" will be at last a hope fulfilled.

www.ingramcontent.com/pod-product-compliance
Lightning Source LLC
LaVergne TN
LVHW020641110826
845149LV00004B/1301

* 9 7 8 1 4 1 8 1 9 0 0 1 9 *